Stress-Free Living

Lt Gen M M Walia

STERLING PAPERBACKS
An imprint of
Sterling Publishers (P) Ltd.
A-59, Okhla Industrial Area, Phase-II,
New Delhi-110020.
Tel: 26387070, 26386209; Fax: 91-11-26383788
E-mail: mail@sterlingpublishers.com
www.sterlingpublishers.com

Stress-Free Living
© 2005, Sterling Publishers Pvt. Ltd
ISBN 978 81 207 5571 0
Reprint 2005, 2006, 2009, 2010

All rights are reserved.
No part of this publication may be reproduced, stored in a retrieval system or transmitted, in any form or by any means, mechanical, photocopying, recording or otherwise, without prior written permission of the original publisher.

Printed in India
Printed and Published by Sterling Publishers Pvt. Ltd.,
New Delhi-110 020.

Contents

Introduction	5
1. The Physiology of Stress	7
2. Food and Stress	14
3. Health and Physical Fitness	19
4. Effective Life Management	40
5. Positive Thinking	49
6. Managing Moods and Habits	56
7. Relaxation – Antidote to Stress	62
8. Meditation – Ultimate Panacea for Stress-Free Living	84
9. Spiritual Approach to Stree-Free Living	90

Introduction

Stress is perhaps the number one problem bothering almost everyone today – the haves as well as the have-nots; the growing and the grown-ups also, as well as the successful and not-so-successful. As a result, 'stress-management' has become a rather popular training and development programme.

There are already a large number of books on the subject of coping up with the problem of stress. Then, where was the need for this little book on the subject? The uniqueness of the book lies in adoption of a 'holistic approach' to dealing with this modern man's worst affliction, wherein a simple, actionable 'action-plan' has been presented to enable one to live a life which is free of stress. Does it sound an impossible proposition?

Although varied psychosomatic manifestations of stress appear mostly in physical, or at the worst level, in psychological forms, yet to be able to eradicate stress fully from one's life, there is a need to go down to the spiritual dimensions too. Going beyond the mental to the spiritual level is an essential prerequisite to enjoy stress-free living.

This book endeavours to challenge the terrible threat that stress seems to pose to the so-called 'modern' lifestyle, by according an integrated perspective in a holistic manner, covering the basic facets of stress – the physical, emotional and spiritual. It also synergises the research of the Western world with the wealth of Oriental ancient wisdom.

The Physiology of Stress

What is Stress?
Stress afflicts almost everyone yet what exactly the word 'stress' means is not so clearly understood. 'Tension' is perhaps its best synonym, while some other expressions such as pressure and strain are also used in lieu. In all these terms, conditions like anxiety, worry, fear or helplessness are axiomatically inherent. Its worst manifestation leads the sufferer to a state of total collapse or deep depression.

To define stress in precise scientific terms is difficult, as its perception varies from person to person. The main reason is the fact that both the cause and effect of stress are mixed up in trying to describe it. The unpleasant situation which causes stress, as also its outcome in the form of anxiety, are both referred to as stress.

The most fundamental genesis of stress lies in the state of failure to achieve what we want to get. We fail to accept the basic fact that all desires may not always get satiated. (May be, it is best this way!) The more the desires are allowed to run amok, the more stressful will our life be; there can be no doubt about this.

That stress is the inevitable result of our way of living today, is yet another misconception. Stress is definitely avoidable even today. However, it needs to be understood that it is not always the external causes which are responsible. The source of stress, more often than not, is internal. So, since 'I' am mostly responsible for landing myself in a state of stress, I should also be able to protect myself from this undesirable state.

In the above context, another allied term, viz 'pressure' needs to be understood. Pressure is essential for one's growth and betterment. It is neither good nor bad by itself. It can lead to the negative phenomenon of stress, or on the contrary, spur faster developmental activity. However, uncontrolled pressure, for a prolonged period, may be counter-productive and should be thus avoided.

The Autonomous Nervous System and Stress

The autonomous nervous system comprises the 'sympathetic' and the 'parasympathetic' nervous systems, which are its two complementary parts. The former responds to the needs of the body during increased activity and in emergencies. The functions of the sympathetic system include speeding up the heartbeat, sending additional blood to the muscles and enlarging the pupils of the eyes to use all available light.

The latter, in general, opposes the action of the sympathetic system. Its functions include slowing down the heartbeat, diverting blood from the muscles to the stomach area and contracting the pupils of the eyes.

When in a stressful situation sympathetic nervous system stimulates the pituitary gland and consequently hormones are released.

These chemical substances prepare the body for stress. It causes a rise in the blood pressure and rate of heartbeat. Muscles also become tense, trying to respond to the 'threat' of stress and hence the speed of conversion of food to energy in the muscles also increases. This sudden and excessive utilisation of the stored up energy has a serious adverse effect on the body.

Fortunately, the body has a wonderful self-restorative process called 'homeostasis', whereby the parasympathetic nervous system takes charge to restore the body to its original balance, and breathing, heartbeat, blood pressure and the digestive system become normal. However, if the stressful situation continues for long or if the balance gets disturbed too often, the homeostatic process may not be able to restore the balance so well. The body will get exhausted and may suffer from reduced functional ability.

Indicators of Stress

Physical Symptoms
- Not bothering about how one looks physically
- Nail-biting
- Sweating
- Dryness of mouth
- Nervous tapping or movement of hands or of legs
- Tired look
- Disturbance in normal sleep pattern
- Excessive tendency to eat and smoke
- Going to toilet far too often

Mental Symptoms
- Losing one's temper excessively or general irritability/aggressiveness
- Worrying about trifles
- Inability to prioritise, concentrate and decide what to do

- Unpredictable moods or unnatural behaviour
- Fear and phobias of over-powering nature
- Loss of confidence in oneself
- Tendency to remain aloof
- Talking too much or becoming totally uncommunicative
- Disturbed memory
- In extreme cases, total breakdown

Adverse Effect on One's Spirituality
- Begin to doubt in existence of God
- Tendency to make mockery of religious practices
- Giving up all spiritual habits such as prayer or going to places of worship
- Running to anybody or everybody for spiritual help

Stress-Related Ailments
- High blood pressure
- Heart disease
- Disturbed digestion, stomach ulcers, colitis, diarrhoea/constipation
- Malfunctioning of the thyroid gland

- Breathing disorders – including persistent cough, asthma or tuberculosis
- Skin disorders
- Headaches – including sinusitis and migraines
- Menstrual problems; miscarriage
- Sexual problems – including impotence
- Miscellaneous psychological problems – including child abuse and wife bashing

It may be emphasised that stress is not a natural outcome of modern lifestyle and is avoidable. Life can be made stress-free by adopting a holistic approach to life management, as elaborated in the subsequent chapters.

Nine De-Stressing Thoughts

- Sense of humour is essential to survive in the stressful modern day environment.
- Recreation is not a waste of time.
- Hard work has never killed anyone – lack of work leading to boredom has.
- Stress is infectious – avoid company of stressful people.
- Choose a job of your liking – work will become a pleasure.

- What cannot be cured must be endured.
- Do not take life too seriously.
- Be ruthlessly objective in accepting criticism from others.
- Whatever happens is for the good – it could have been worse!

Food and Stress

Type of Food

We are what we eat. The type of food we eat has both immediate and long-term effect on us, at all the three levels – the body, mind and spirit. Food which is *tamasik* (ie stale or leftover) in nature is bound to generate stress as it tends to upset the normal functioning of the human body. Fresh food, whenever available, must be preferred. Excessive use of condiments should be avoided. Taking piping hot tea/milk or steaming hot food also disturbs one's usually calm attitude. Further, it is a mistaken belief that smoking or drinking, even in moderation, relieves stress. Simple meals with one or two food items, rather than too many lavish dishes, are advisable. Thus, vegetarian diet is preferable. Although it is customary to serve fruits with food, it is not the right thing to do. This is because different kind of digestive secretions are produced by the stomach for variant foods. Mixing up too many varieties of food items at one meal creates avoidable problems for the digestive system. In fact, any one type of fruit, preferably taken in the morning, is better.

The Quantity of Food

On an average, we eat almost three to four times the quantity of food that we actually need. A lot of body's energy is used up for digesting the excess food. It is said that after a particular level of food intake, the 'food actually eats one up'.

It is always good to eat a little less than your 'full-stomach' capacity. Besides, never eat food unless you are really hungry. Having dinner at 8 or 9 pm, after a heavy snack at 5 or 6 pm in the evening is asking for trouble. In fact, skipping an odd meal is always good if the stomach is upset. There are varying views on the benefits of fasting, but we will not discuss them here. However, giving a break to one's stomach, at least once a week, by having only fruit or milk, etc, may be worth trying.

While a little bit of water taken with meals is all right, drinking too much water with food is not advisable. Water, taken an hour or so before or after meals, is good for digestion.

One's diet must be balanced with all the required nutrients for a healthy living. Also remember, excess of everything is bad. Related to the problem of stress, excessive intake of salt is definitely out. Too much of sugar, fried food and chillies are not good either. Overindulgence and excessive craving for a particular taste/type of food generates *rajasik* (aggressive) or at worst, *tamasik* (dull) tendencies.

Intake of Food

An even more important aspect of the relationship between food and stress lies not so much in what or how much we eat but how the food is taken. For example, food eaten in great hurry or in a state of anger or any other negative state of mind, is bound to induce stress.

How the food is served is also very important. Not only the presentation, cutlery, crockery, etc play a role, the love and affection with which the food is served is also significant.

Finding faults with food while it is being eaten is the worst habit. It is better not to eat the food you do not like, rather than finding fault with it.

It is good to have regular food habits. Workaholics who do not find time to eat food at proper mealtimes are inviting stomach ulcers.

One must try to enjoy one's food, and therefore, eating at the so-called lunch/dinner meetings is highly inadvisable. Every morsel of food should be enjoyed with a totally peaceful state of mind. Food and discussions should not be mixed.

There are accepted ways to 'charge' the food we eat. Prayer is perhaps the best method for energising the food and it will do some definite additional good at no extra cost!

Water Intake

While we consume over four times the food our body requires, the water intake is almost one-fourth, particularly in winters. Lack of adequate quantity of water in the body causes serious damage to our entire system.

Four glasses of water, preferably stored in a copper utensil for twenty-four hours, taken first thing in the morning helps in easy flushing of the toxins from the system. The water must be gulped and not sipped so that it goes straight into the intestines. One may start with drinking one glass of water initially and gradually increase the intake in a couple of weeks. This gets rid of the problem of constipation.

Water taken during the rest of the day must be slowly sipped and not gulped so that it is absorbed in the region of stomach. When we talk of water intake, it means water and not other beverages, like soft drinks and tea. In fact, the habit of taking chilled aerated drinks with food is not good for digestion. It is like pouring cold water on fire!

The relationship between food and stress may not appear very clear and direct to you now but it undoubtedly exists. The body sustains on the energy that food provides to it. The mind will be calm or agitated depending on the state of body. It is, therefore, important that food and water are given due consideration for stress-free living.

Nine Simple Ways to Minimise Stress at Work

- Be reasonable with your ambitions.
- Do not try to be a 'winner' all the time.
- Avoid being too much of a perfectionist.
- Learn to occasionally forgive yourself (and, of course, others too).
- Be realistic in allocating time for any activity.
- Acquire the ability to say 'no' without hurting anyone.
- Set apart some time for yourself when you are 'not available' for phone calls/visitors.
- Do not insist on doing everything yourself. Delegate!
- Avoid following 'No Mistake' syndrome. To err is human, to forgive is divine.

Health and Physical Fitness

Keeping Fit

Maintaining a general state of well-being and making efforts to keep oneself physically fit is an essential prerequisite for coping with stress. Regular practise of *yogasanas* is highly beneficial. Five Tibetan exercises have been recommended in this chapter. These five yogic *kriyas*, as they may be called, are an extremely effective way of energising the *chakras* (energy centres) for maintaining good health.

The Art of Proper Breathing

The air that we breathe contains oxygen. Nobody can live without it for more than a few minutes. Yet most of us do not breathe properly. We are used to 'shallow breathing', in which we use only two-third of our lung capacity; the remaining one-third, just above the ribs, remains clogged with carbon-dioxide. The correct way of breathing is 'abdominal breathing', wherein we breathe through the stomach vis à vis the lungs. When we make use of the diaphragm while breathing, full capacity of the lungs is used in inhalation and exhalation.

The extra intake of oxygen can do wonders to improve one's general health. It will take about a week's consistent effort to correct one's faulty breathing habit, to switch from shallow to abdominal breathing. To start with, lie down on the bed and keep a book on the stomach. Now, when you breathe, if the book noticeably moves up and down in the breathing process, the method is correct.

If you have noticed, newborn babies always breathe abdominally – slowly and properly. Unfortunately, gradually they also take to the faulty way of breathing.

Lastly, *pranayama*, one of the most important components of *Ashtang Yoga* (Eightfold Path of Yoga*), is all about proper breathing. If one is keen, the technique can be learnt from a qualified teacher.

Body Posture

The body posture that we adopt while standing, sitting, walking or lying down is of vital importance. Without being stiff, the spinal column must always remain straight. Shoulders should not droop forward. The neck also must remain in normal central position rather than it being bent forward, backward or to any one side.

Most important point to be noted is that one's body must remain comfortably straight while sleeping in the bed. Soft/sagging mattress must be avoided as it is one of the leading causes of backache. A hard bed is the best option.

Use of thick pillows is one of the major causes of cervical spondylitis. Using no pillows or only very thin ones is advisable.

Regular Exercise

Spending at least twenty minutes a day in following a physical exercise regime that suits you is a must. Exercises which generally stretch and strengthen various muscles of the body must be regularly practised. Besides, the *yogasanas* offer a wide choice of exercises to tone up your entire system – particularly the nervous system, which is an important factor in dealing with the problem of stress.

The following section outlines some simple yogic *kriyas* for daily practice. They will take just about 15 to 20 minutes of your time.

Last, but not the least, morning walk is one of the simplest, efficacious and enjoyable exercise. Do accord sometime for it.

Five Tibetan Exercises

This brief section describes five ancient Tibetan exercises which help promote better health and vitality. These exercises are yogic kriyas developed by the Tibetans. If performed regularly, they will produce tangible improvements in your personal life within a short period of thirty days.

Besides being simple, these exercises can be done at any place and under all climatic conditions. They can be adopted by anyone who wishes to maintain good health and attractive personality.

Principles of 'Yogic' Kriyas

It is a well-known fact that the body has seven principal energy centres corresponding to the seven major endocrine glands. These are called the 'chakras'. The hormones produced by these glands regulate all our bodily functions. Medical research has convincing evidence that even the gradual deterioration of body cells and organs is controlled by these hormones. The yogic kriyas regulate the body's seven energy centres and maintain the hormonal balance. This makes one feel younger day by day.

In a healthy body, the energy centres or chakras spin at a great speed in the clockwise direction, enabling vital life energy, also called the *pranic* or etheric energy, to flow upward through the endocrine system linked with these chakras. But, if one or more of these chakras begin to slow down, the natural flow of energy is locked. This is the main cause of ill health and the aging process.

The quickest and the easiest way to ensure good health and, arrest or at least slow down the aging process is to make these energy centres spin normally once again, through daily practice of the five yogic kriyas mentioned here.

The benefits of these exercises come only if practised regularly. Devoting about twenty minutes a day to do these exercises in the morning or evening is worthwhile.

Please ensure that you have warmed up by doing some simple limbering-up exercise before you start. Avoid doing these exercises immediately after having food or when your stomach is full.

Kriya No. 1
- Stand erect with the arms outstretched, horizontal to the floor. Now, spin around clockwise until you become slightly dizzy.
- In the beginning, practise the exercise only to the point of slight dizziness. With time, as you practise all the five exercises, you will be able to spin for a longer duration without feeling dizzy.
- In order to lessen the dizziness, before you begin to spin, focus your vision on a single point straight ahead of you at the level of your eyes.

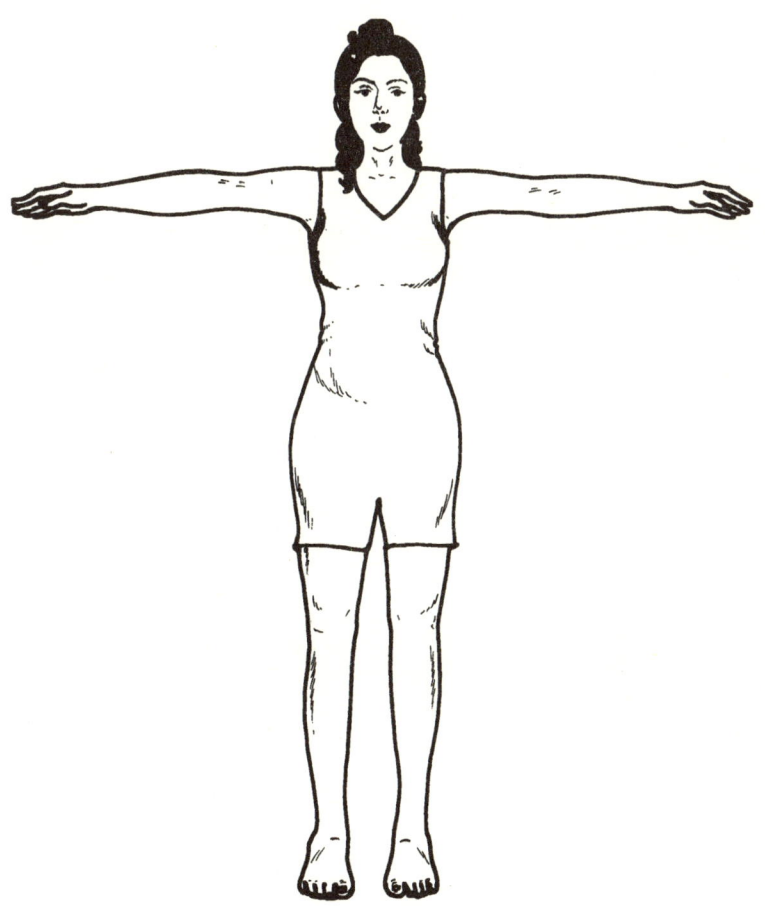

Kriya No. 1

Kriya No. 2

- Lie flat on a carpeted floor, face up. Fully extend your arms along your sides and place the palms of your hands against the floor, keeping the fingers close together. Then, raise your head slightly off the floor, tucking the chin against the chest. (This chin-lock is important). Now lift your legs, keeping the knees straight, into a vertical position. If possible, let the legs extend back over the body, a little towards the head, but avoid bending the knees.
- Then, slowly lower both the head and the legs to the floor keeping the knees straight. Allow all the muscles to relax for a while, and then repeat the exercise.

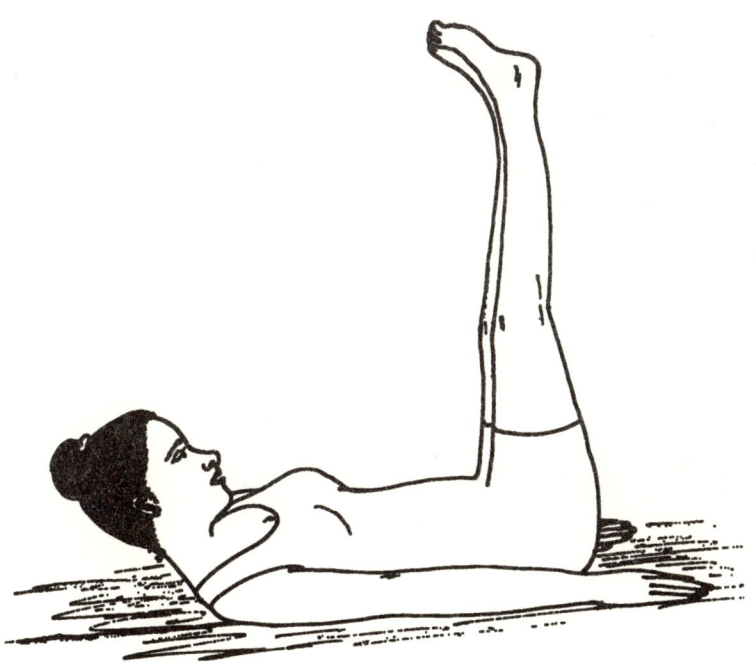

Kriya No. 2(a)

- With each repetition establish a breathing rhythm. Breathe in deeply as you lift the legs and the head and breathe out as you lower them. Even when relaxing, continue breathing in the same pattern. The more deeply you breathe, the better.
- If you are unable to keep the knees perfectly straight initially, let them bend as much as necessary. But, as you continue to perform the kriya, gradually attempt to straighten them as much as you can.

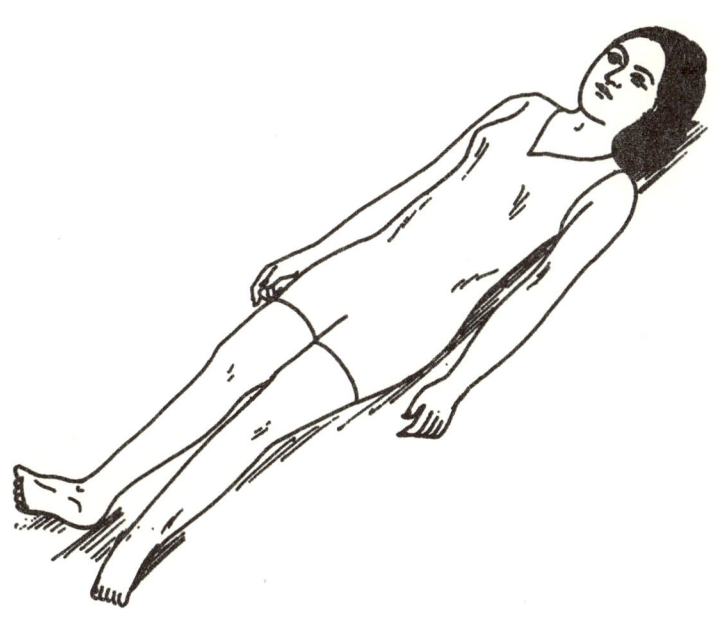

Kriya No. 2(a)

Kriya No. 3

- The third kriya, which should be practised immediately after the second one, is very simple. Kneel on the floor with the back straight and the body erect. Place your hands along your sides.

- Slowly bend the head forward, tucking the chin against your chest. Then, bringing it slowly to the original position, bend it backwards as much as you can. At the same time, arch the spine backwards. As you do so, reach out for the ankles and hold them for support. Now, return to the original position and start the exercise all over again.

- In this kriya too, you should establish a rhythmic breathing pattern. Breathe in deeply as you arch the spine and breathe out as you return to an erect position. Deep breathing is most beneficial; so take as much air into your lungs as you possibly can.

Kriya No. 3

Kriya No. 4

- Sit on the floor with your legs straight out in front of you and your feet about one foot apart. Keeping the back straight, place the palms of your hands on the floor, alongside the buttocks (fingers pointing to the front). Then, tuck the chin forward against your chest (chin-lock).
- Next, bend the head backwards as much as you can. Simultaneously, raise your body, so that the knees bend but the arms remain straight. The trunk of the body and the upper legs will be in a straight line, horizontal to the floor; both the arms and lower legs will be straight up and perpendicular to the floor.

  Now, tense every muscle in the body for two-three seconds. Relax them as you return to the original position, and rest a while before repeating the procedure.
- Breathing rhythm is equally important in this exercise. Breathe in deeply as you raise the body. Hold in your breath as you tense the muscles. Breathe out as you return to the sitting position.

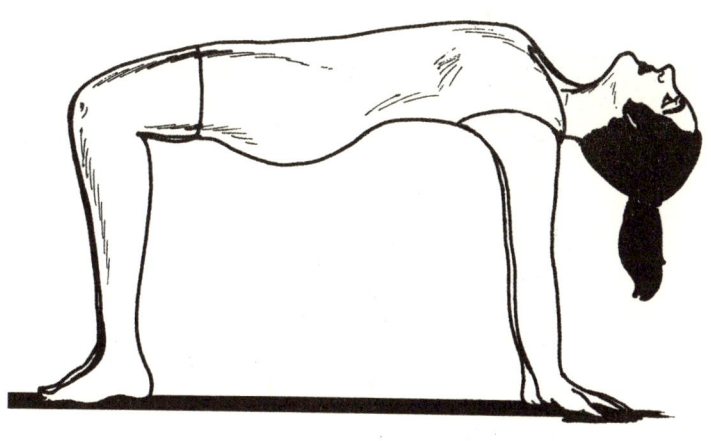

Kriya No. 4

Kriya No. 5
- Lie face down on a carpeted floor. Bend your arms at the elbows and place them palm down, near your face. Keep your feet about two feet apart, and the toes flexed. Balancing your weight on your hands and keeping the legs straight, raise your body and arch the spine backwards. Now, bend the head backwards as far as possible. Then, raising the hips, bring the body up into an inverted 'V'. At the same time, bring the chin forward, tucking it against the chest. Return to the original position, and repeat the exercise.
- Follow the same deep breathing pattern used in the previous kriyas. Breathe in deeply as you raise the body and breathe out fully as you lower it.

Guidelines
- To start with, practise each kriya three times a day for the first week. With every week that follows, increase the daily repetitions by two, until you are performing each kriya twenty-one times a day.
- It is okay if you need time to increase the frequency of any particular kriya. You can do so gradually.

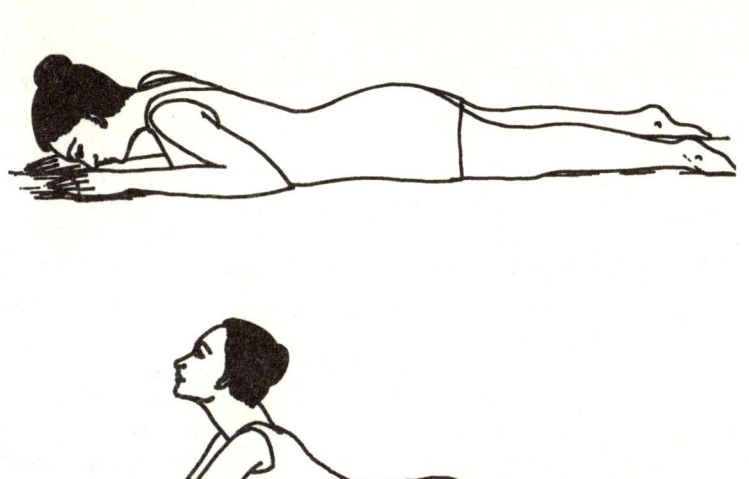

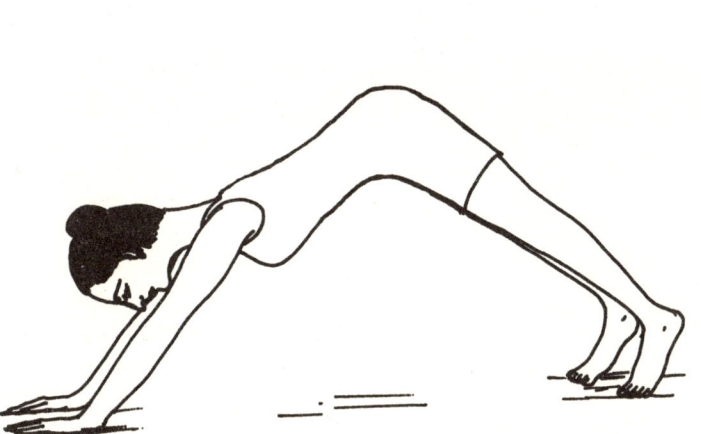

- These kriyas can be performed in the morning or in the evening, whenever it is convenient. After about four months, apart from performing them the full number of times in the morning, perform just three repetition of each *kriya* at night. Gradually, increase these to twenty-one as well.
- The five kriyas are interconnected with each other, and all are equally important. If you find that you are not able to do all of them the required number of times, try splitting them into two sessions, one in the morning and one in the evening.
- Under no circumstances should you ever strain yourself. That would be counter-productive. Start with as much as you can handle and build up gradually. And never be disheartened. With time and patience you will succeed.
- These kriyas are so effective and result oriented that even if one were left out while the other four were practiced regularly, excellent results would still be experienced. Even one kriya alone will do wonders!
- If you already have some kind of exercise programme, you may continue it. Though, a yogic exercise programme not only tones up the

nervous system, it helps the body in maintaining a youthful equilibrium. In fact, the five kriyas help in activating the energy centres, and the body becomes even more receptive to the benefits of the other exercises that you do.

- Deep, rhythmic breathing while resting between repetitions of the kriya is important. In between each of the kriyas, it would be helpful to stand erect with your hands on your hips, breathing deeply and rhythmically several times. As you breathe out, imagine all the tension draining out from your body, allowing you to feel quite relaxed and at ease. As you breathe in, imagine that you are filling yourself with a sense of well-being and good health.
- Lastly, do not take a cold water bath after the exercise – even in summer. Tepid water will be good.

Remember, you are as old as you think. One's mental attitude makes all the difference. If you are able to see yourself as a young man, in spite of your advancing age, others will also see you that way. Once you begin practising the kriyas, you are making an effort to remove from your mind the image of yourself as a weak old man. This proves to be a very strong auto-suggestion.

A lot of people may find it difficult to change the way they see themselves. They are convinced that the body is programmed to, sooner or later, become old and feeble, and nothing can be done to alter this course of Nature. These kriyas will help them change their mindset.

Timely Medication

While it is possible to maintain a general state of good health through a balanced diet and regular exercise, need for medical attention must not be ignored. Effort must be made to first cure the ailment through the process of self-healing or Nature Cure. If need be, alternative treatments such as Acupressure, Reiki, Siddha-Sciences, Homeopathy or Ayurveda can be adopted. Resort to Allopathy only in acute/serious cases. What system of medicine is adopted is not so important, as long as it gives lasting results, without creating bigger complications in the long term.

In the final analysis, please remember that even 5-10 minutes of exercise just before a bath will do wonders to your health. So, do find at least this much time, for your sake!

Nine Easy Ways to Avoid Stress at Home

- Always remember, a stress-free home contributes to your success in life in a big way.
- Avoid bringing 'work' from office to home.
- Do not carry the unpleasantness of the workplace with you to your home.
- Remember, you do not continue to be the boss at home. Play your appropriate role of father/mother or husband/wife when you return.
- Do not allow discussions to turn into arguments. Always patch up after a tiff with your spouse before going to sleep.
- Appreciate gestures of goodwill, however small. Ignore minor irritants and avoid faultfinding in others.
- Plan your budget – enjoy living within your means.
- Avoid comparisons.

Effective Life Management

A purposeful and well-planned life, wherein time is not frittered away over inconsequential trifles and in brooding over the past or worrying about the future is most desirable to remain stress-free. How this can be effectively managed is the purpose of this chapter.

The Purpose of Life

A macro view of the purpose of human existence is the most essential first step to make one's life meaningful. The aim/objective of life will axiomatically flow from this broad philosophy.

Moksha, which literally means 'liberation' from worldly shackles and merging with the Divine, may be the ultimate in this context, particularly for a highly evolved spiritual person. For a layman, however, it may not make much sense. Nevertheless, the term *moksha* can become meaningful for an ordinary mortal when used in the context of getting rid of one's demonic traits and imbibing divine qualities. *Moksha* is, thus, achievable even in one's present life.

The best answer to the question – 'What is the purpose of one's life? – which I got from the students of class XI/XII of a school and appeals to me the most, is, *"To generate all-round happiness."*

In the above context, just to be happy myself cannot be the purpose of life, for I cannot be really happy unless I make others happy too.

Core Values

Life, which is based on the primary dictates of righteous conduct (*Dharma*), requires strong foundation to be able to withstand the routine stress and strain without much hassles. These core values must be inculcated by parents and teachers in the formative years of a child.

All religions have a more or less similar ethical/moral code. From these, a guiding philosophy must be evolved, outlining certain basic principles which must be kept in view in managing one's life. Nine of them, the more important ones according to me, are listed below:
- Fearlessness
- Link between fate, karma and destiny
- Non-attachment
- Desirelessness
- Avoidance of hypocrisy
- Non-violence
- Patience

- Faith
- Humility

Planning One's Life

Most people would like to believe that it is not possible to plan one's life in today's world. If one asks a child today as to what would he like to become when he grows up, he is quite at a loss to give a coherent answer. The usual cryptic response will be 'it depends'. It depends on what? Should it not depend on you and primarily you alone?

If my life depends on others and not basically me, I am bound to become the so-called 'victim of circumstances' and my life will undoubtedly be stressful.

Setting Achievable Goals

These if evolved in a pragmatic manner are a prerequisite for making one's life worthwhile. These objectives or goals must cover the periods of one's life as shown below:-

a) Long-term goals   10-15 years
b) Mid-term goals   3-10 years
c) Short-term goals   6 months to a year

While long-term goals concern the ultimate purpose of life, short-term goals are of immediate concern and thus it is very important to plan them out. These could be broken down into monthly, weekly and daily goals which need to be achieved by meticulous planning.

Long-term goals, once properly evolved by deep consideration, must be adhered to and followed up vigorously by achieving middle and short-term goals.

Crisis Management

At some time or the other in life, everyone has to face a crisis – whether at a personal or a professional level. Of course, the best thing to do is to take timely action to diffuse the circumstances which may build up to a level of crisis. Most crises are, thus, avoidable.

However, if the situation does go out of hand, as sometimes it may, do not close your eyes to impending threatening indicators. Early detection and timely response to deal with it with all the vigour is the best option.

If a crisis of a grave dimension threatens to disturb you beyond reasonable limits, do remember, every crisis has a lifespan. It cannot last forever. So, continue to deal with it till it is fully overcome.

Also, do not forget to carry out a 'critique' at the end of it all so that useful lessons for the future are learnt from it.

Management of Time

Inability to manage time is one of the most crucial causes of stress in life. It is, therefore, of paramount

importance to find time for activities such as those given below to be able to ward off stress and have a more enjoyable life:
- Enjoying your meals
- Exercising
- Taking rest and relaxing
- Reading what you love
- Practising silent contemplation
- Enjoying with spouse/children
- Recreation
- Serving the needy
- Praying

Major Energy Centres (Chakras and Their Characteristics)

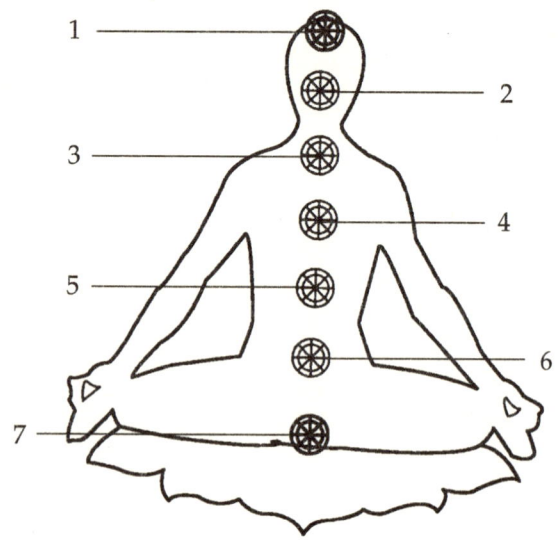

Sr. No. (Chakra)	Energy Centre	Associated Colour	Associated Endocrine Glands	System	Parts of Body Governed	Sense	Element	Emotional Psychological Functions
1	CROWN (*Sahasradal*)	Violet	Pineal	-	Upper brain, Right eye	-	Spirit	Connects with Spiritual self.
2	THIRD EYE (*Adnya*)	Indigo	Pituitary	Nervous	Lower brain, Left eye, Ears, Nose	Intuition (Sixth Sense)	Thought	Intuition Centre. Visualisation and thought forms. Being practical in life.
3	THROAT (*Vishuddha*)	Blue	Thyroid, Parathyroid	Respiratory	Throat, Lungs, Bronchial apparatus	Sound	Ether	Communication centre. Accepting and assimilating.
4	HEART (*Anahat*)	Green	Thymus	Circulatory	Heart, Lungs, Liver, Hands	Touch	Air	Love and compassion. Openness to life.
5	SOLAR PLEXUS (*Manipur*)	Yellow	Pancreas, Adrenal	Digestive, Nervous	Stomach, Liver, Gall Bladder, Spleen	Sight	Fire	Self pride and wisdom. Self connection with universe.

Sr. No. (Chakra)	Energy Centre	Associated Colour	Associated Endocrine Glands	System	Parts of Body Governed	Sense	Element	Emotional Psychological Functions
6	HARA (*Swadhisthan*)	Orange	Gonads	*Reproductive*	Male and Female Reproductive System	Taste	Water	Connected with Being of self, Emotion, Feelings.
7	ROOT (*Mooladhar*)	Red	Adrenal, Supra Renal	*Excretory*	Kidneys, Bladder, Spinal Column and Legs	Smell	Earth	Sea of Kundalini enemy. Quality of relating to opposite sex – Physically, Mentally, Spiritually. Being grounded with self.

Difference between Urgent and Important

Avoidable stress is suffered because of not prioritising things in order of their importance and urgency they deserve. Daily checklist of things must be categorised into 'Must Do', 'Should Do' and 'Could Do' – things in the order of their importance.

Differentiating between the 'urgent' and 'important' activities is crucial. Urgent things are those which must be done immediately. For example, crucial, time bound projects, SOS health problem, etc. On the other hand, important things generally concern the long-term goals or even high priority short-term goals. For example, planning, recreation, exercising etc. The following points in this regard are noteworthy:

- For successful life management, it is of paramount importance that adequate time is accorded to things which one considers important.
- Things which are both urgent and important must be given the highest priority.
- Urgent things may well be delegated to others to handle quickly.
- Do not waste time on things which are neither urgent nor important.

Nine Tips for Better Time Management

- Do not postpone urgent and important activities.
- Do not let the clock chase you. (You cannot hurry up by repeatedly looking at the watch!)
- Delegate things that are neither very urgent nor important.
- Do not try to do everything at once – learn to prioritise.
- Concentrate on one thing at a time.
- Stick to a planned time schedule.
- Organise your place of work, office table and files.
- Designate 'Prime Time' exclusively for yourself and let your imagination run amok.
- Let go of the attitude of 'hurrying up' all the time.

Positive Thinking

"Think positive ... the rest will follow."

– Saheb

Positive thinking is the key to a healthy and stress-free living. Positive thoughts have a powerful influence on one's attitude. These invariably lead to positive action. In fact, the genesis of good action lies in positive thinking. Thus, all negative emotions should be kept at bay.

The Power of Thought

Since all thoughts originate from the mind, purity of mind is a prerequisite for pure and positive thoughts. The faculty of 'thinking' is perhaps one of the greatest gift human beings have. The powerful influence these thoughts have on one's personality and attitude is indeed phenomenal.

Every impulse of the mind converted into thoughts is conveyed to the body cells. If there is any negativity in these, they will lead to confusion, depression and resultant stress. The body's defence mechanism gets adversely affected and may totally break down in an extreme situation. Thoughts are thus, the creator of dynamic, vital and subtle forces.

Positive Mental Attitude

Keeping the mind constantly engaged in positive thinking will help in fulfilling one of the greatest requirement for an effective personality – the Positive Mental Attitude (PMA). A man with a PMA will look for good in every situation; this will help him maintain a serene and calm attitude irrespective of the circumstances.

Given below are simple ideas on how to acquire and maintain a PMA.

Accept Life as a Package Deal

There is not a single person in the world who has only a good future or bad luck comprising his experiences in life. By and large, the sum total of life's goodies or hardships in everyone's life, when seen dispassionately, is the same.

This Too Shall Pass

Connected with the above, it is worthwhile to note that there is nothing permanent in life. Both fortunes and misfortunes have a lifespan. So, there is no need to be excessively jubilant when life is full of smiles, nor is there any need to believe that the end of the world has come when everything seems to go wrong.

Both the phases of life are temporary. So, when the going gets tough, there is no need to break down.

Differentiate between an Event and a Problem

Life is indeed a series of events, not a continuation of problems. Let us, therefore, not look at every event as a problem. For example, arranging the marriage of one's son/daughter should be treated as an event, not a problem. Similarly, a child's admission to the school is not a problem. Life will go on and events will keep on happening. This is universal.

Convert Every Challenge into an Opportunity

Let me tell you a story – a true story, to illustrate my point. Long, long ago, the boss in Bata Company sent his two sons from Yugoslavia to Canada, to promote sales. The elder son went to the east coast and the younger one to the west. Both found the situation in their respective areas equally bad. The elder son, after surveying the market, sent the following note to the head office:

"People hardly wear shoes here. No scope for selling shoes. Stop dispatch of any consignment."

The other son, who found the situation equally dismal in the west coast, sent the following report:

"Not many people wear shoes. Tremendous scope for promoting sales here. Request double the consignment of shoes being dispatched."

Given above is a classic example of looking at a glass of water as 'half-empty' or 'half full'. Interestingly, the word 'empty' sends a negative thought and the word 'filled' sends a positive thought to the mind.

Search for Good in Others
No human being, however useless that person may seem, is totally good for nothing. The art of managing people lies in locating that goodness in them which is not so clearly visible. The most sacrosanct and bounden duty of parents and teachers is to search for the hidden talent in their wards and then taking all measures to develop the unique attributes they are endowed with.

If this did not happen, Einstein – adjudged as the greatest personality of the last century – would have been rearing sheep for a career!

Whatever Happens Is for the Better
(It is true, believe it or not!)

The apparent misfortune – a bolt from the blues – may have bigger gifts in store. Always keep the window open for Divine Grace to enter and fill the empty coffers in Her own mystic way.

Always Expect Good Results
This philosophy is based on the infinite power which lies in one's subconscious mind. *Yad bhaavam tad*

bhavati. "As the man thinketh – so he becomes." If one sows seeds of success in the mind, he will reap success and the same applies to failure. An optimist expects good news and generally 'good luck' favours him. Whereas, a pessimist is always scared of disappointment, if what he hoped for did not actually come through. People who are called 'accident prone' are not only careless while driving but they are most likely to be afraid of accidents, which they keep visualising in their minds all the time.

Count Your Blessings, Not Misfortunes
Ordinary mortals that we really are, always keep cursing our lot for what we do not have (and worse still, what the neighbour, who we think does not deserve, has). We actually forget so many goodies that life has offered us and which a very large number of people actually do not have. It is often said – one is unhappy not as much because of his own misfortunes as he is of someone else's fortunes.

A boy who was cursing himself for not getting a new pair of shoes for his birthday, felt quite ashamed to see a child who had no feet!

Further, as a practical guide, try to build on your assets rather than eradicating the liabilities from your personality traits. The former is much easier!

Do not curse the destiny by branding it "bad". It could be worse!

Get Out of the 'Kaliyug Syndrome'

If you call the period of time we live in Kaliyug, how can you expect anything better than what you are getting in return? Can you imagine what Lord Rama himself would have gone through when his better half was taken away by Ravana during the *Satyayug*. The ordeal of Sita during her captivity in Lanka, worsened later, as the result of a *dhobi's* silly remarks regarding her chastity, in the context of stress and strain can hardly be described.

Therefore, to say that stress is an unavoidable part of the modern times, and that it was not there in the good old days, is questionable.

Look at the luxuries that the modern science has provided us with. Almost everything is within easy reach of an average man today. Is not this a great *yug* then? *The mind is its own place, and in itself/Can make a Heaven of Hell, a Hell of Heaven*. It is for the individual to decide what s/he wants.

Nine Points for Stress-Free Driving

- See that your vehicle is well-maintained and is fit for the journey.
- Before starting on a journey, ensure that proper documents, toolkit and a can or bottle of water, etc all are there in your vehicle.
- Do not let your vehicle run on 'reserve'. Fill it up!
- Over-speeding is stressful. Be gentle on your accelerator.
- Start early to reach the destination well in time.
- Do not insist on always having 'right of way'. Take it easy if the driver of the vehicle in front of you does not readily give you a pass to overtake.
- Do not indulge in serious discussions or arguments while driving.
- Practise 'relaxation' on 'Stop' signals at crossings.

Managing Moods and Habits

The dictionary meaning of the word 'habit', is 'a thing that you do often and almost without thinking'. The key word here is 'often'.

Continuous repetition of a habit will make it more and more firmly ingrained in one's nature. In this case, it becomes very hard to uproot it. As one can see, if the letter 'H' is removed from HABIT, A BIT remains. On removing 'A' BIT is still left and after removing 'B' IT would still remain. *Habits are easy to acquire and tough to get rid of.*

Moods are yet another facet of attitudes which cause stress in one's life. Remaining in a good or bad mood is also a matter of habit. These are not dictated by external factors or behaviour of others, as is mostly believed. They are an outcome of one's own thinking from within, perhaps as a reaction to an outside influence.

The first thing in this regard will be to see that we do not pick up a bad habit. Secondly, we must learn to insulate ourselves from all external influences which disturb our mental equanimity.

Following is a list of some good habits which will enable us to have a healthier and stress-free life:

Early to Bed and Early to Rise
Of course, this will make one 'healthier, wealthier and wiser' as the saying goes. But unfortunately, the modern generation does exactly the opposite and yet hopes to have good health. Late nights, if allowed to become the order of the day, can never help in achieving stress-free living.

Doing More than What You Are Paid For
This helps in reducing the mercenary approach to life and strengthens your ability to enjoy work, which is a prerequisite for stress-free living.

Replacing 'Competition' with 'Cooperation'
Excessive spirit of competition causes unnecessary stress. The best competition is when you compete with yourself and push your inherent potential to produce better and better results. Combining the spirit of competition with cooperation is, of course, the best option.

Forgive and Forget

Human beings are gifted with these two beautiful qualities. Carrying a heavy burden of hatred and revengefulness is the cause of many a psychosomatic ailments. Use of the word 'sorry', more so when it is backed up by sincerity, is an excellent antidote to strains and tensions in mutual relations. We often continue to recall things not worth remembering but forget those precious little mercies which must never be forgotten.

Avoid Arguments

Pleasant discussions may slowly turn into acrimonious arguments if one's 'ego' is allowed to have an upper hand. It is best to listen more and talk less. Find areas of agreement rather than disagreement in discussions. Everyone is entitled to have his own point of view, which need not disturb your ego. Besides, there are various ways to do a particular thing. Adopting a win-win approach is the ideal solution.

Express Gratitude

The habit of expressing one's gratefulness through the use of a simple word like 'thanks' is perhaps the best. There cannot be a more effective method of acquiring peace of mind, so essential for keeping stress and tension at bay. There are indeed innumerable things happening in one's life for which there is need to express genuine gratitude to people or God, everyday.

Avoid Jealousies

Do not harbour the feeling of jealousy for anyone. What the other person gets is part of his/her destiny. Whether or not they deserves it, is not for you to judge. Besides, it is not that their good luck is at your cost. The person you are jealous of may not even be aware of it. You are also not in a position to deprive them of the good luck. The only thing that you certainly are doing is harming yourself!

Smile More

Laughing is, undoubtedly, the best medicine, but there is no tonic which is more invigorating than a smile. Make a habit of going to sleep wearing a smile, irrespective of how good or bad was your day. It's wonderful to make it a habit of waking up in the morning wearing a smile on your face. Keep smiling, particularly in times when smiling is not so easy. It may not be so easy, but surely it is the most effective antidote to stress.

Do at Least One Good Deed a Day

Make it a habit to take stock of the day's events before you go to sleep at night and ascertain as to what is it that you have done during the day that you can be proud of and call it a 'good act'. If you cannot think of any such act, try reading a passage from the scriptures that you are fond of, saying a short prayer, or ringing up a friend who needs your support. Cumulative goodwill that one is bound to collect like this is astounding in content. It will come to one's rescue in some terrible situation.

Moods and Habits Linkage

The subtle linkage between moods and habits clearly exists. Getting into a good or a bad mood or being known as a 'moody' person is definitely not an attribute of an amicable personality. One can get into the habit of becoming moody and thus become unpredictable or can remain calm and composed during both rough and smooth times. Besides, by being in a bad mood, one does more harm to one's own self than to others. To learn to avoid being moody is an essential prerequisite for living a stress-free life.

Nine Steps to Relieve Stress
(Five Minutes a Day)

- Gaze at the rising sun every morning. (Do *Surya Namaskar*, if you like!)
- Lie down in a quiet place (roof or somewhere in the garden) and watch the clear sky or the clouds drifting by.
- Appreciate the beauty of a flower.
- Talk to an ailing person to cheer him/her up.
- Sing or hum your favourite tune.
- Talk to your pet.
- Talk to a baby – also give him/her a hug.
- Wear a smile and talk to yourself, standing in front of a mirror.
- Observe total silence *('mauna')* of the body, mind and spirit.

Relaxation – Antidote to Stress

The pace and tempo of modern life leaves little time for relaxation. An almost unbroken daily schedule of tense activities and long hours of work cause stress and strain and lowering of both physical and mental fitness.

It is thus necessary to take measures to not only relieve this tension but also to make optimum use of the energy produced by the body, so that we can perform our duties with more alertness, less fatigue and a relaxed frame of mind.

A relaxed individual will react more spontaneously and his reactions will be faster in any emergency. A person learning to drive, for example, tires after just 15-20 minutes of driving, whereas an experienced driver can drive hundreds of miles effortlessly because his mind and body are relaxed.

Relaxation and Its Threefold Manifestation

Total relaxation is a combination of physical, mental and spiritual relaxation and is essential to overcome the daily stress and strain. These are as mentioned below:

Physical Relaxation

This implies relaxation of the entire body, that is the limbs and muscles as well as the internal organs such as heart, lungs and so on. It is achieved through a process of auto or self-suggestion, transmitted to each part of the body, telling it to relax. Starting from the toes, it moves gradually upwards to the ears and eyes, taking each limb in turn. Similar messages are then sent to the internal organs.

Mental Relaxation

Mental tension brought about by fear, anxiety and fatigue takes a heavier toll than the physical fatigue. The simple way to ease one's mental tension is deep rhythmic breathing. This implies concentration on slow and deep inhaling and exhaling, which produces a feeling of bliss and contentment in a short time.

Spiritual Relaxation

This is a product of physical and mental relaxation, and is induced by 'cutting' oneself from all other thoughts except of oneself. The mind is 'emptied' of all that is around us, including the body. A feeling of great calm and peace is achieved thereby.

Relaxation Exercises

Stress and strain, as a result of long and continuous tension, without much opportunity for sports or other recreation can be harmful by way of reduced efficiency as well as health problems. This can be prevented and overcome to a large extent by carrying out the relaxation exercises as explained and illustrated in the following pages.

These exercises can be done individually or in a group at any convenient time and place. It is not necessary to do them in one continuous session. They can be done selectively, depending upon the situation and the time available.

Stretching Exercises

The stretching exercises are a series of simple postures meant to make the body more flexible. Actually, 'exercises' may not be the best word, for these are done slowly and gently, for relaxation, rather than for strengthening.

Most of us find that our neck becomes tense and stiff due to prolonged stress. Head rotations are a simple way to begin relaxing the neck and shoulder and can be done anywhere, at any time, as explained in the following steps:

- Sit comfortably in a chair or on the floor and inhale. (The exercise can be done while standing also, but some people find it hard to keep their balance while doing it.) Gently move your neck backwards.

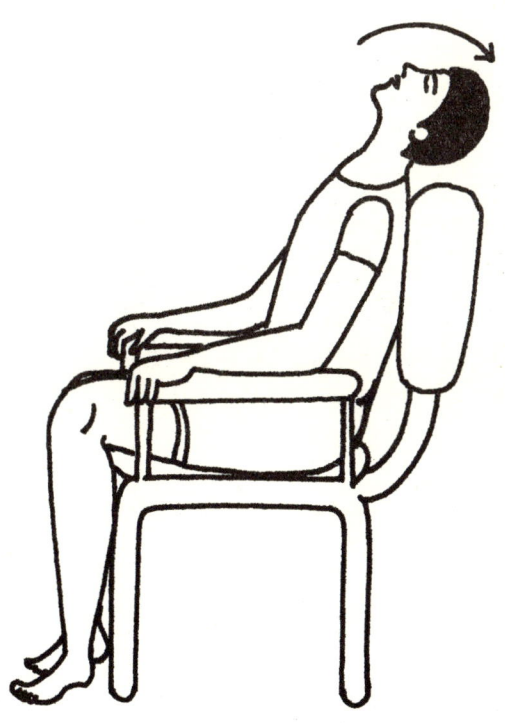

- Exhale slowly and bring your head down as close to your chest as you find comfortable. Pressing the chin to the chest (chin-lock) is ideal.

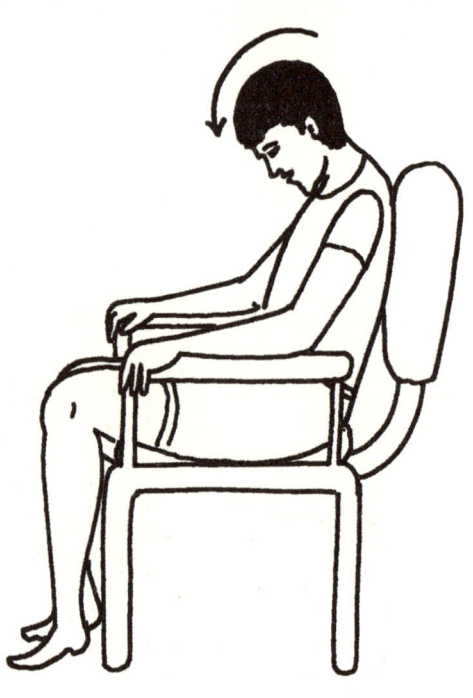

- Feel the gentle stretch on the back of your neck and in your shoulders. Bring your head back to the centre and relax.

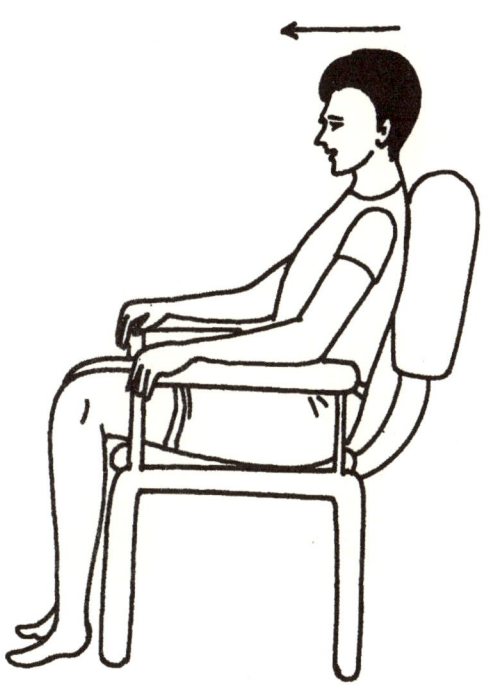

- Inhale slowly and turn your head sideways to the left. Pause for a few seconds.

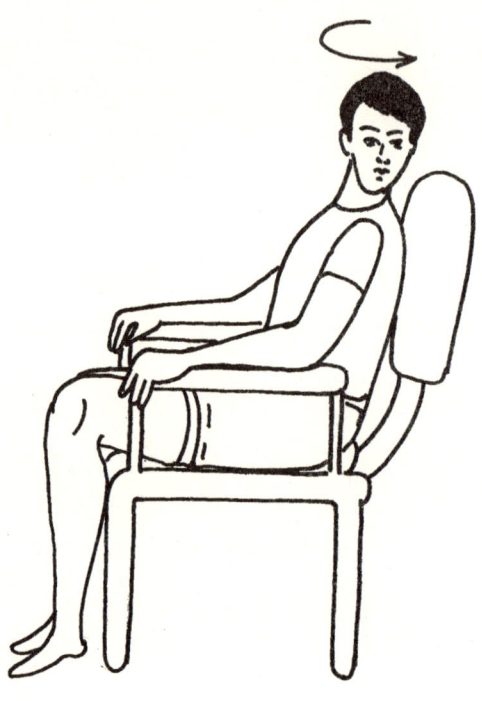

- Exhale and return to the original position.
- Turn your head sideways to the right now. After a pause, return to the normal position.

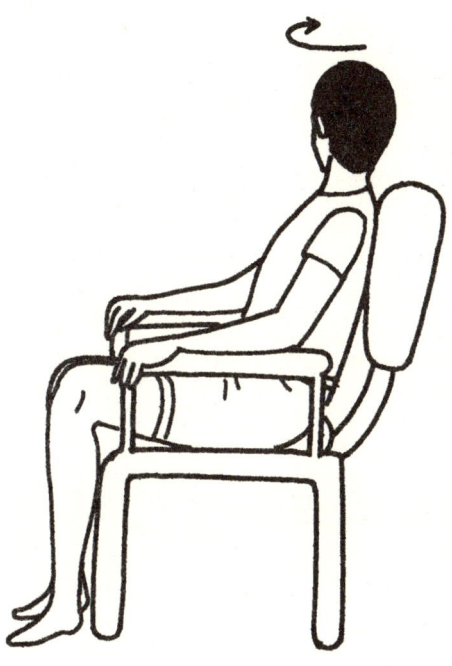

Following are some exercises you can perform seated on a chair with your back straight:

Head Rotations

Inhale as you slowly bend your head towards your left shoulder. Avoiding any jerky movement, swing your head backwards and relax your jaw. Exhale

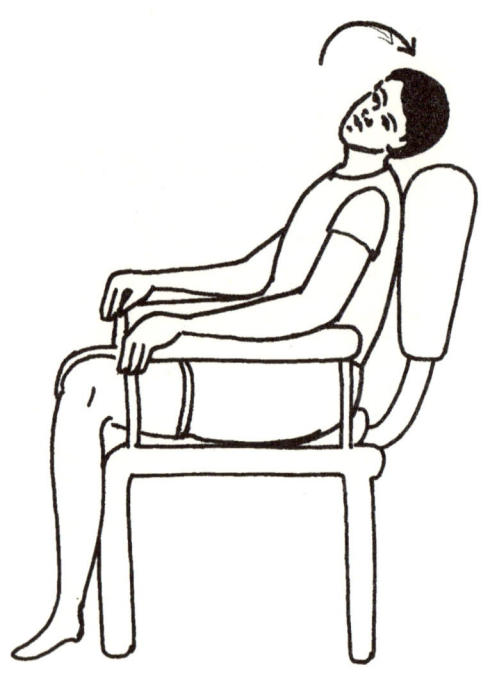

slowly and bring your head towards your right shoulder, then bend it forward to make a chin-lock. Continue till you return to where you started from.

This completes one anti-clockwise head rotation. The clockwise head rotation can be done similarly, starting from your right shoulder.

Shoulder Rotations

Raise both your shoulders towards your ears. Now slowly rotate them backwards and bring them lower

first, and forward later. Repeat the exercise in the opposite direction now.

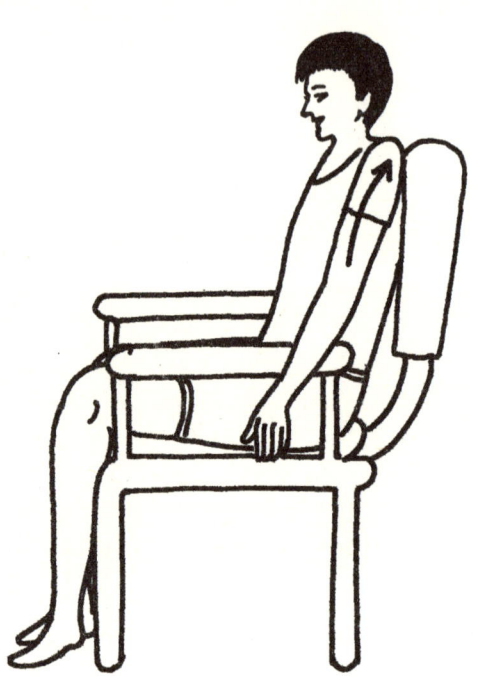

Spinal Twists

Sit at the edge of your seat with your back straight, or stand erect. Twist the upper half of your body to the left first, and then come to the original position before twisting the body to the right. Return to the original position once again.

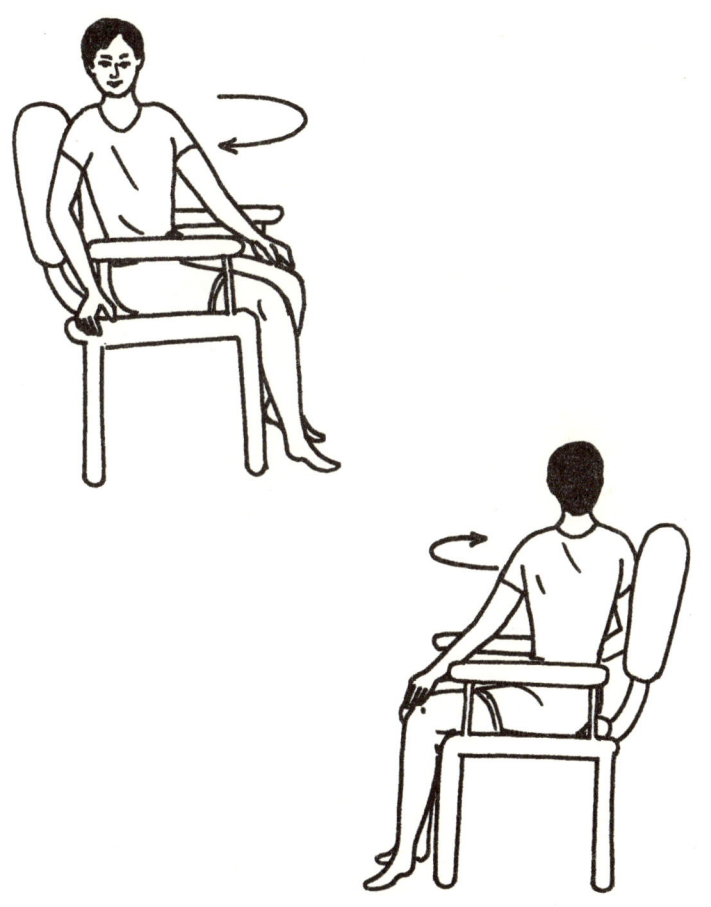

Forward Stretches

Sit on a sturdy chair, towards its front edge, with legs and feet slightly apart. Inhale as you slowly bend forward, allowing your shoulders and arms to sag between your knees and feet. Pause for a few seconds, exhale and slowly return to the sitting position. Avoid any jerky movements.

Stretching Your Lower Back

Inhale slowly and lift your left leg, bringing it parallel to the floor as much as possible. Bring it back to the

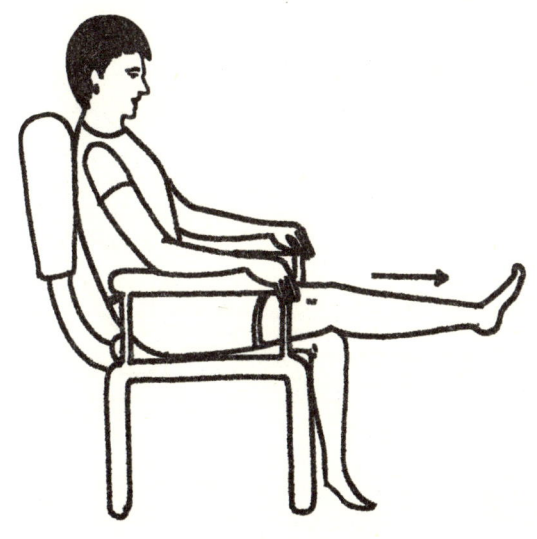

normal position. Repeat the same with your right leg now. Do not strain to keep the leg parallel. You will manage to do so with practise.

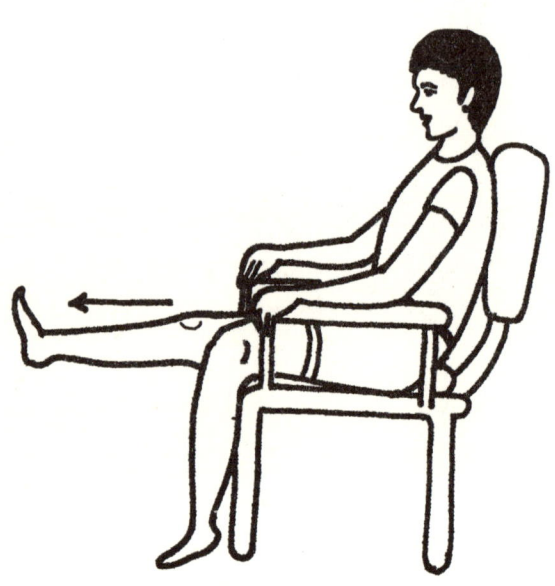

Rotating Your Ankles

Stretch your left leg forward and raise it slightly above the floor. Rotate your foot from the ankle in an anticlockwise direction first, and then in a clockwise

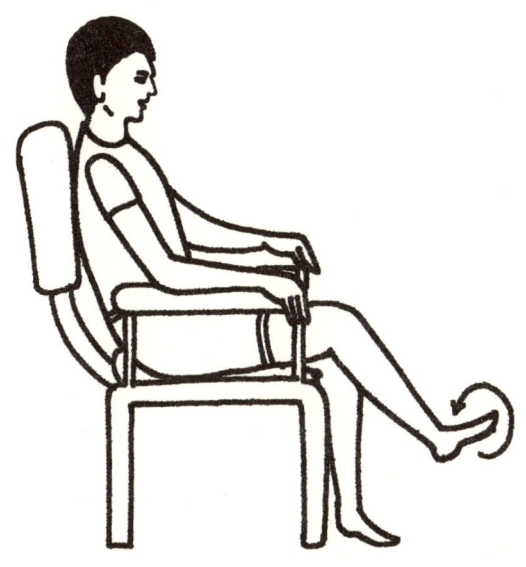

direction. Lower the leg and repeat the same with your right leg.

Each of the above exercises should be done 4-5 times initially. The number of these repetitions can be increased gradually over a period of time.

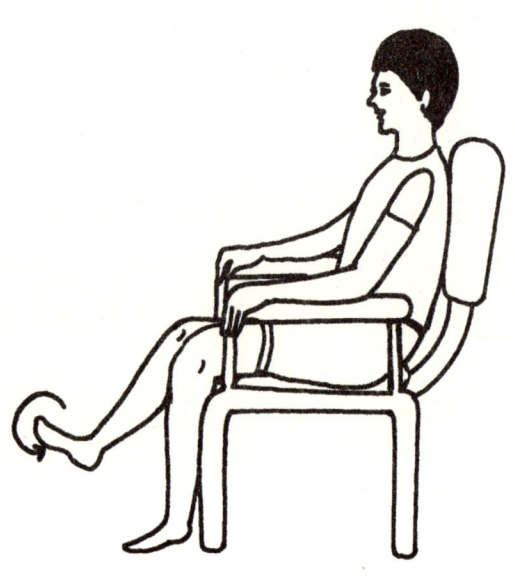

Shavasana

Shavasana, for deeper relaxation, is also known as the 'corpse' posture. This technique is simple yet very powerful, and diffuses calm, peace and harmony around you. It is excellent for inducing sleep.

Technique

- Lie comfortably on your back with your eyes closed. Try not to move. The legs are placed slightly apart, the arms lie gently alongside the body, hands turned up or slightly inwards, fingers half closed.
- Starting from the feet, relax each part of the body. Inhale deeply and slowly. Concentrate on your breathing. As the inhalations become deeper, imagine yourself taking in lots of pure oxygen.

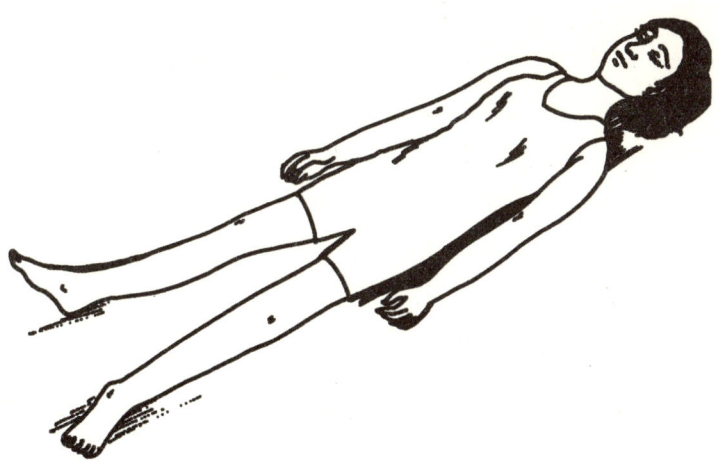

With each exhalation, imagine all impure air from your body being expelled.

- You can also lie down comfortably sideways such that one leg lies over the other and both the knees and the ankles touch each other.

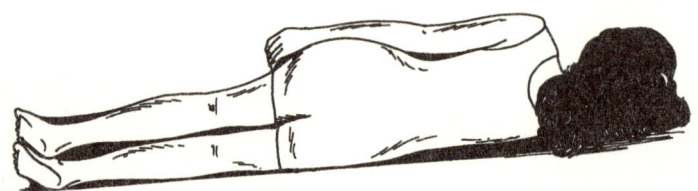

Conclusion

Relaxation and laziness are not synonymous terms. In fact, your body and mind function most efficiently and effectively when you are relaxed. Thus, these techniques can help you achieve more with the same or less effort. All techniques described here are restorative and can be extraordinarily useful for better health and general wellbeing.

Nine Habits that Help in Living a Stress-Free Life

- Learn to adjust with circumstances that you cannot change.
- Learn to say 'no' without feeling guilty.
- Learn to look for something good in apparently bad situations.
- Learn to say 'sorry' even if it is not your fault.
- Learn to forgive and forget.
- Learn to ignore remarks you do not deserve.
- Learn to often laugh it off.
- Learn 'to agree to disagree'– sometimes.
- Learn to unlearn some bad habits.

Meditation – The Ultimate Panacea for Stress-Free Living

Yogic meditation is perhaps the greatest gift given to the modern man, the value and usefulness of which are eternal. Ideally, its practise should be part of the *Ashtang Yog*. (See next chapter for details).

Meditation

Meditation is that state of mind where there is perfect union of the self and the higher-self, or the conscious and the subconscious state of mind. In the final analysis, when one's individual soul (*jeevatma*) has established total linkage with the Universal Soul (*Parmatma*), one is in perfect state of meditation.

Samadhi is a step forward in the spiritual journey, when *Atma* and *Parmatma* merge in each other just like a drop of water does in the ocean.

There are numerous ways in which meditation can be taught and practised, although the essential aim remains the same.

Cybernetic Meditation

Cybernetic meditation is 'goal-oriented'. It goes beyond the usual practice of meditation that concerns itself with the achievement of a blissful state of mind, which in any case, is the prelude to cybernetic meditation. The goal here is to achieve a long lasting stress-free state of mind.

A simple technique which explains the method of always remaining in our natural, stress-free state is outlined in the succeeding paragraphs.

Technique

- Sit comfortably on a chair, or lie on the bed with your spinal column straight but not stiff. Close your eyes.
- Wear a gentle smile. It activates your thymus and makes this exercise more effective.
- Resting your hands on your knees, touch the forefingers to the thumbs, forming the *gyan mudra*. If lying prostrate, rest your hands along your sides, on the bed. This posture acts like a 'switch-on' for the meditation process.
- Relax each part of the body, starting from the top of the head to the toes, visualising them mentally.

- Gently roll up your eyeballs, without opening your eyes, and activate the command and control centre of your entire nervous system.

- By visualising and relaxing your internal organs, much deeper relaxation is achieved.

- Lastly, concentrate on your breathing for about five minutes, wherein your attention is on the nostrils. Feel the cool, clean air, full of oxygen, going in, and the slightly warm air carrying all the impurities being exhaled. Be a relaxed witness to the complete process.

- Experience a sort of weightlessness. Imagine you are floating in the air. Auto-suggest your inner self to 'let go'.

You have now reached the state in which your subconscious mind will be able to register auto-suggestions from your conscious state of mind and do whatever you want it to do for you.

After surrendering to the subconscious mind, concentrate once again on your breathing. With every exhaled breath, imagine stress being expelled as 'blue smoke'. Inhale the power of relaxation coming into your body as white-coloured light. Do this exercise for about two to three minutes.

It is time now to complete the process of Cybernetic Meditation with an expression of gratitude for having being relieved from stress.

Rub your hands together and place the palms over your eyes. Gently moving them outwards, visualise yourself to be stress-free. Send the following auto-suggestion to your subconscious mind for best results by saying – "When I open my eyes at the count of five, I will be totally stress-free."

Now, gently open your eyes, with a smile on your face and a belief that you are really stress-free. Faith in the process will do miracles!

Although the technique of Cybernetic Meditation could be practised any time of the day, for best results it can be done just before going to sleep – for about 20 minutes to start with and for a lesser duration of time with more practise. The visualisation part is preferably done first thing in the morning when you open your eyes. This has the advantage of the subconscious mind working for you for 6-8 hours while you were asleep. Besides, the ritual of doing it at a fixed time will ensure that you do not forget it. It will also help you in getting sound sleep and you will wake up full of life the next morning.

Cybernetics is an extremely effective tool to achieve everything you deserve. And you undoubtedly deserve a stress-free life.

Nine Quotable Quotes

- I can't change the direction of the wind, but can adjust my sails.

    – Anonymous

- There are two things to aim at in life: first, to get what you want; and after that, to enjoy it. Only the wisest of mankind achieve the second.

    –Logan Smith

- To be wronged is nothing unless you continue to remember it.

    –Confucius

- Am I not destroying my enemies when I make friends of them?

    –Abraham Lincoln

- A life full of error is not only more honourable, but more useful than a life dedicated to doing nothing.

    –George Bernard Shaw

- Life is either a daring adventure or nothing.

    –Helen Keller

- You can have everything in life you want, if you will just help enough other people get what they want.

    –Zig Ziglar

- People are lonely because they build walls instead of bridges.

  –*Newton*

- All forms of stress and illness are lessons in love. They are consequential symptoms of absence or lack of love, either for yourself, for others or from others.

  –*Robert Holden*

Spiritual Approach to Stress-Free Living

In the concluding chapter, the ultimate answer to deal with the problem of stress will be discussed. In a nutshell, it can be said without doubt that a life which is truly spiritual will not have even an iota of stress. In fact, the genesis of stress lies not so much in the body or the mind, it is mainly in the soul.

Spiritual Life

Firstly, it needs to be understood as to what exactly is meant by 'spirituality'. The root word 'spirit' or soul *(atma)*, which is the most important component of all living beings, owes its origin to the ultimate source of spirit viz, *Parmatma*.

The fundamental question 'Who am I?' can be discussed for hours. But in the simplest terms, the answer is 'I am I'. The Vedantic truth – *Aham Brahm Asmi* – implies that 'I am a temporarily separated entity of God. But I am not something very different from Him.' More precisely, "I am *Sat-Chit-Anand*."

If *Anand* is the essential part of what I am, how can there be ever anything wrong with me – at the physical, mental and spiritual level?

The next question that can be put to oneself is – "What is the purpose of my life?" If we believe in what the Bible says – "Me and my Father are One", then the purpose of our life cannot be variant to what God's aim of creating us is. *Anand* is the essential ingredient of this purpose – generating and spreading happiness all round which will also ensure our own happiness.

Our Enemies Within

To be able to lead a spiritual life which is healthy and tension free, we must first know our six enemies inside us, as also how to deal with them.

These could be broadly categorised as 'selfishness' or 'excessive I-consciousness'. The root cause of all these is 'desire'. It gives rise to 'anger' and 'jealousy' in case of failure to achieve what we want, and 'attachment' if we succeed. Excessive attachment leads to 'greed', which, when satisfied, gives way to 'conceit'.

The six enemies laid bare above cause all the stress and strain in life. The only way to deal with these 'masters' – as Sri Sathya Sai Baba calls them – is to control our desires. And that can be done by following the path of perfect yoga.

Eightfold Path of Yoga (*Ashtang Yog*)

Following from the above, control of desire and not letting it run amok, is the first and foremost prerequisite for keeping the mind at peace. *Ashtang Yog*, by Rishi Patanjali, is the ultimate path to stilling the agitations of the mind. The essence of the path is outlined as follows.

First Step: Control of the senses (*yama*). This includes non-violence (*ahimsa*), truth (*satya*), non-stealing (*asthya*), celibacy (*brahmacharya*) and non-acceptance (*apari-graha*). It means giving up attachment with the body and over indulgence in senses. Excessive joy in good times and deep sorrow in even minor troubles must be avoided as part of dealing with day-to-day happenings.

Second Step: Control of passion (*niyama*). Purity (*soucha*), contentment (*santosha*), penance (*tapas*), self-study (*swadhyaya*) and surrender to God (*Ishwarya parnidham*) are its basic ingredients. *Niyama* is essentially unconditional love for God.

Third Step: Mastery of posture (*asana*). Steady posture of body and mind (both steadiness at physical level and inner tranquility) is essential.

Fourth Step: Regulating the breathing process (*pranayam*). *Prana* is the vital life-force, which sustains through rhythmic deep breathing.

Fifth Step: Withdrawal of senses (*pratihar*). Inward withdrawal of the five senses, working through the five sense organs (*gyan-indriyas*) – the tongue, eyes, ears, skin and the nose, is *pratihar*.

Sixth Step: Concentration (*dharana*). When the mind acquires an undeviating attitude towards one eternal truth viz., God, that is real *dharana*.

Seventh Step: Meditation (*dhyan*). Experiencing that One and only One, eradicating all other thoughts, is the real meditation.

Eighth Step: Complete consciousness (*samadhi*). When the person who is engaged in meditation forgets both himself and the fact that he is in meditation, he experiences *samadhi*.

Conclusion

All agitation (of mind) will cease the moment one enquires, "Who am I?" This was the *sadhana* Ramana Maharishi achieved and taught to his disciples. This is also the easiest of all disciplines. It requires underplaying the body consciousness to the extent possible and reiterating the essential truth that "I am I". This requires a spirit of total surrender to Him.

Nine Spiritual Guidelines for Stress-Free Living

- You have right (*adhikar*) only on your duty (*karma*), to do your best, not on the results (*phalam*) thereof.
- Notwithstanding the above, good acts will invariably lead to good results. 'One reaps as one sows'.
- Nobody has the right (or ability) to disturb your peace of mind – without your permission (which must never be granted).
- Nothing happens without a cause; your own behaviour/actions may be part of the cause. So, do not curse your luck.
- Though you are the creator of your destiny (a sum total of your past and present *karmas*), everything that you get or do not get in life is dictated by destiny itself.
- Neither good nor bad luck is perpetual.
- Helping the needy, whether or not he deserves your help is the best insurance against stress.
- How can you fail if you make **Him** your partner in all your endeavours?
- Why **worry**, when you can **pray**?

Suggested for Further Reading

1. Stephen Williams, *The Positive Approach to Stress*, Rajendra Publishing House, Mumbai.
2. Vera Peiffer, *Stress Management*, Thorsons Harper Collins Publishers.
3. Peter Kelder, *Fountain & Youth*.
4. Jose Silva, *The Silva Mind Control Method*, Pocket Books.
5. Dr Joseph Murthy, *The Power of Your Subconscious Mind*, Bantam Books.
6. Pt. Shambhunath, *Stress Management Through Yoga & Meditation*, Sterling Paperbacks.
7. Swami Satyananda Saraswati, *Yoga Nidra*, Yoga Publication Trust (Munger - Bihar)
8. Pramod Batra, *Simple Ways to Managing Stress*, Tink Ince.
9. *Beyond Stress*, (Vol VIII, No. 2), Mananam Publication series, Chinese Mission.